THE WORLD'S BIGGEST
INSECTS

by Mari Schuh

pogo

Ideas for Parents and Teachers

Pogo Books let children practice reading informational text while introducing them to nonfiction features such as headings, labels, sidebars, maps, and diagrams, as well as a table of contents, glossary, and index.

Carefully leveled text with a strong photo match offers early fluent readers the support they need to succeed.

Before Reading

- "Walk" through the book and point out the various nonfiction features. Ask the student what purpose each feature serves.
- Look at the glossary together. Read and discuss the words.

Read the Book

- Have the child read the book independently.
- Invite him or her to list questions that arise from reading.

After Reading

- Discuss the child's questions. Talk about how he or she might find answers to those questions.
- Prompt the child to think more. Ask: What is the biggest insect you have ever seen?

Pogo Books are published by Jump!
5357 Penn Avenue South
Minneapolis, MN 55419
www.jumplibrary.com

Library of Congress Cataloging-in-Publication Data

Schuh, Mari C., 1975- author.
 The world's biggest insects / by Mari Schuh.
    pages cm. – (The world's biggest animals)
Summary: "Carefully leveled text and engaging full-color photos introduce early fluent readers to the world's biggest insects, describing their physical features and behavior while comparing aspects of their size to everyday items familiar to young readers. Includes activity, glossary, and index."–Provided by publisher.
 Audience: Ages 7-10
 Includes index.
 ISBN 978-1-62031-208-7 (hardcover: alk. paper) –
 ISBN 978-1-62031-260-5 (paperback) –
 ISBN 978-1-62496-295-0 (ebook)
 1. Insects–Size–Juvenile literature. 2. Insects–Juvenile literature. I. Title.
 QL467.2.S374 2016
 595.7–dc23
                                                    2014050220

Series Editor: Jenny Fretland VanVoorst
Series Designer: Anna Peterson
Photo Researcher: Anna Peterson

Photo Credits: Alamy, 7, 20-21; Getty, 4, 10-11; Minden, 18-19; Nature Picture Library, 8-9, 12-13, 15, 16-17; Shutterstock, cover, 1, 5, 6 14, 23; Thinkstock, 3.

Printed in the United States of America at Corporate Graphics in North Mankato, Minnesota.

TABLE OF CONTENTS

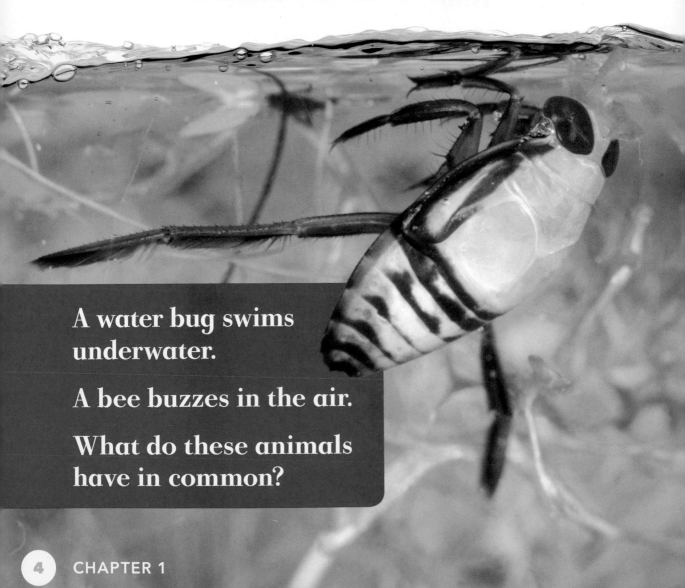

CHAPTER 1

WHAT ARE INSECTS?

A water bug swims underwater.

A bee buzzes in the air.

What do these animals have in common?

They are both **insects**. Insects are small animals with six legs.

An insect's body has three parts. Most insects have wings and **antennas**.

antenna

leg

wing

CHAPTER 2

LONG
AND THIN

Stick insects are the longest insects in the world.

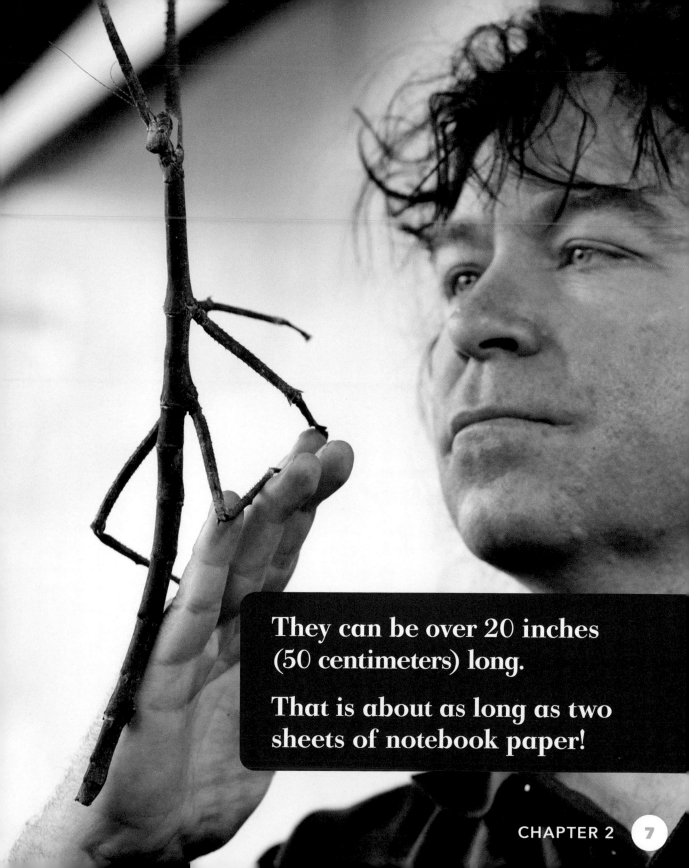

They can be over 20 inches (50 centimeters) long.

That is about as long as two sheets of notebook paper!

Stick insects are long and thin. They look like twigs. Many stick insects are green or brown.

Stick insects hide during the day. They stay still. They blend in with the leaves and branches.

Sometimes they sway back and forth. They look like twigs moving in the wind.

DID YOU KNOW?

Not all stick insects are supersized. Some are very small. One kind of stick insect is just a half inch (12 millimeters) long!

That's smaller than a penny!

antenna

leg

At night, stick insects find leaves to eat. They use their long antennas to smell and feel.

Stick insects have long legs that point in different directions.

A stick insect can shed a leg if a **predator** grabs it. A new leg will grow in its place!

DID YOU KNOW?

Stick insects are also called walkingsticks. But some of these bugs can do more than just walk. They can fly! Some stick insects have wings. They keep them tucked close against their body.

WHERE ARE THEY?

Stick insects are found around the world. They live in forests, **grasslands**, and **tropical forests**. Most stick insects live in warm areas.

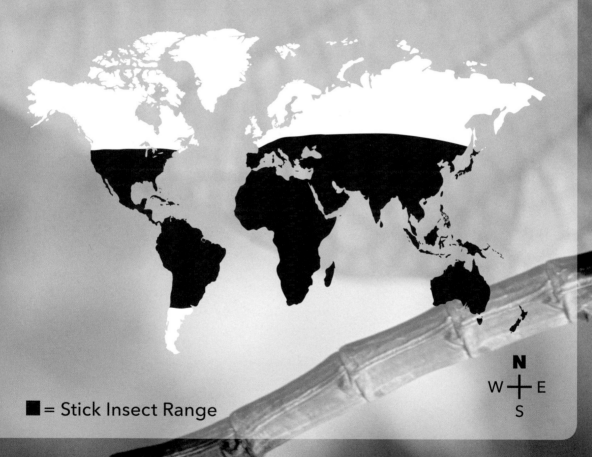

■ = Stick Insect Range

N
W + E
S

Stick insects are the world's longest insects, but many big insects live around the world.

The goliath beetle is shorter than a stick insect, but it has a heavy body.

CHAPTER 3

BIG AND WIDE

Goliath beetles are one of the world's heaviest insects.

They can weigh 3.5 ounces (100 grams).
That is more than three mice!

Goliath beetles are big bugs. They can be more than four inches (10 cm) long. That's longer than a deck of cards.

Beetles have two hard wings that cover two soft wings.

Most beetles lift their hard wings to fly with their soft wings. But goliath beetles keep their hard wings flat.

They slide their soft wings out from the side to fly.

DID YOU KNOW?

A goliath beetle's wings are bigger than a **sparrow's**!

soft wing

hard wing

4 in (10 cm)

Goliath beetles are strong insects.

They have strong legs with sharp **claws**. Their claws help them climb trees.

Males use their horns to fight other males.

DID YOU KNOW?

Goliath beetles are heavy because their bodies have lots of muscle. This muscle helps them lift up to 850 times their own body weight.

That's like you lifting 55,000 pounds (25,000 kilograms)!

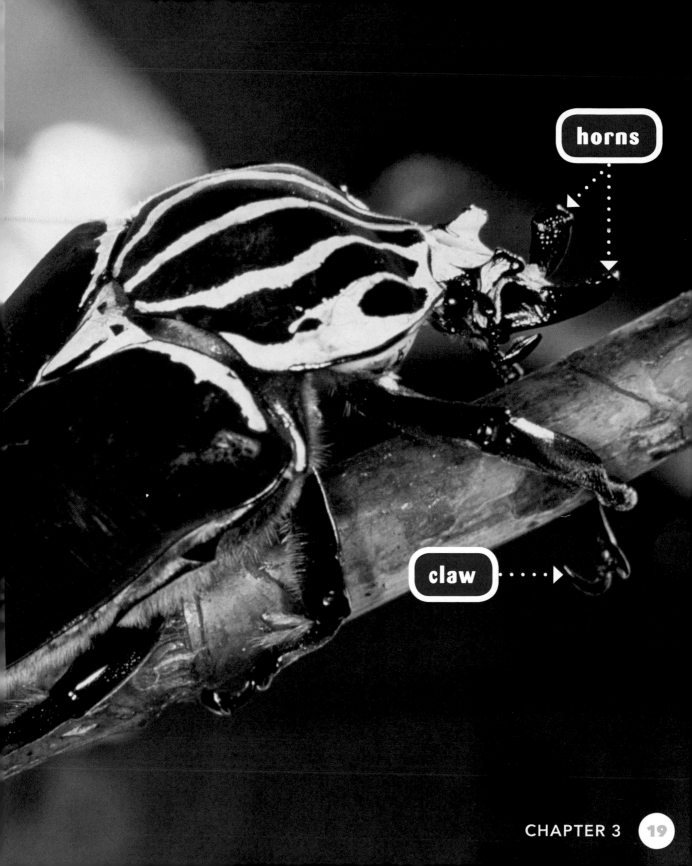

horns

claw

WHERE ARE THEY?

Goliath beetles live in central and western Africa. They live in **rain forests** and grasslands. They eat sweet foods such as **nectar**, **sap**, and fruit.

AFRICA

■ = Goliath Beetle Range

N
W ┼ E
S

Huge goliath beetles fly with their big wings. Long stick insects hide in the trees.

What is the biggest insect you have seen?

ACTIVITIES & TOOLS

HOW LONG?

One stick insect can be as long as five goliath beetles.

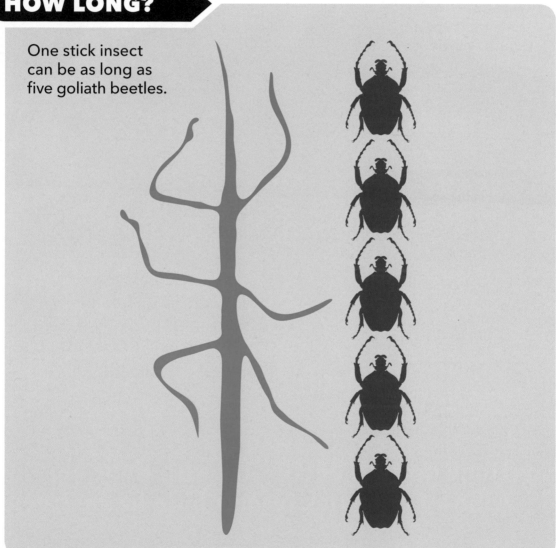

1. **Measure the length of a pencil.**
2. **Now weigh the pencil. Have an adult help you.**
3. **Now measure and weigh other items, such as a toy car, deck of cards, or a shoe.**

Was the longest item also the heaviest? Was the shortest item the lightest? How does an item's length relate to its weight? Or doesn't it?

GLOSSARY

antenna: A body part used to smell and feel.

claws: Sharp, usually thin and curved nails on the toes of an animal.

grasslands: Land covered with grasses rather than shrubs and trees.

insect: A small animal with six legs and three body parts.

nectar: A sweet liquid given off by plants.

predator: An animal that eats other animals for food.

rain forest: A thick area of trees where a lot of rain falls.

sap: The fluid part of a plant that carries food and nutrients.

sparrow: A small bird.

tropical forest: A warm area with a lot of trees.

INDEX

TO LEARN MORE

Learning more is as easy as 1, 2, 3.

1) Go to www.factsurfer.com

2) Enter "biggestinsects" into the search box.

3) Click the "Surf" to see a list of websites.

With factsurfer, finding more information is just a click away.